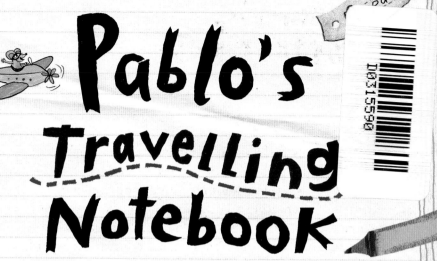

Pablo's Travelling Notebook

Written by Suzanne Torres

Illustrated by Christiane Engel

OXFORD
UNIVERSITY PRESS

OXFORD
UNIVERSITY PRESS

Great Clarendon Street, Oxford, OX2 6DP, United Kingdom

Oxford University Press is a department of the University
of Oxford. It furthers the University's objective of excellence
in research, scholarship, and education by publishing
worldwide. Oxford is a registered trade mark of Oxford
University Press in the UK and in certain other countries

Text © Oxford University Press 2015
Illustrations © Oxford University Press 2015

The moral rights of the author have been asserted

First published 2015

British Library Cataloguing in Publication Data
Data available

ISBN: 978-0-19-835670-7

10 9 8 7 6 5 4 3 2 1

Paper used in the production of this book is a natural, recyclable product
made from wood grown in sustainable forests. The manufacturing process
conforms to the environmental regulations of the country of origin.

Printed in China by Hing Yip

Acknowledgements

Series Advisor: Nikki Gamble
Illustrated by Christiane Engel
Designed by Caitlin Ziegler

Chapter 1

The Adventure Begins

Pablo was flying to Peru to visit his aunty and uncle, Tia Carla and Tio Bruno. He was sitting in seat 9B, feeling very excited.

I love being on this big plane. I just wish I didn't have to sit next to Lola!

Lola was Pablo's little sister. She always asked too many questions. In fact, she looked as if she was going to ask a question right now.

"Pablo ..." she began.

"Not again!" Pablo thought.

"Which is the most special place?" Lola continued. "The UK or Peru?"

"Hmm," said Pablo, frowning. "That's tricky. I love the UK. I mean, we live there, don't we? But Peru is **amazing!**"

Pablo loved visiting Tia Carla and Tio Bruno in Peru. Last time he'd visited, they had gone to the rainforest. Pablo remembered paddling a small canoe on the river with his aunty and uncle, and hearing monkeys in the treetops.

Pablo also recalled how they'd walked through the jungle. He'd found a vine hanging from an old tree and it was so much fun swinging on it. Then he remembered how funny it was trying to get into a hammock without falling out!

"Pablo," said Mum, "we've still got a long way to go. Would you like your new notebook?"

"**Great idea!**" replied Pablo, grabbing his notebook from his backpack.

"Pablo ..." said Lola.

"Not now, Lola," replied Pablo. "I'm busy. I'm going to write in my notebook."

THE MOST SPECIAL PLACE **EVER!**
by Pablo

Ernie the Explorer went to Peru and found his three favourite things.

1. A real **volcano!**

Ernie hiked in the mountains, met a llama, climbed an enormous volcano and then rode down it on a mountain bike.

A bumpy, bumpy ride!

BIKE HIRE

SEAT 9B

2. Awesome **clothes** and **music**

Cool tunes!

Ernie knitted some colourful socks, learned to play the pan pipes and joined a band of musicians.

3. Rainforest **adventures**

Ernie paddled a small canoe, fell out of a hammock (six times!) and swung on a jungle vine.

Ouch!

ERNIE'S TRIP RATING: PERU IS **AMAZING!**

It was night-time when Pablo finished writing in his notebook. He snuggled up under his blanket and fell into a deep sleep. He completely missed breakfast. And he didn't see one of the cabin crew fold up his table and put his notebook into the seat pocket in front.

When Pablo woke up, they'd landed.
He was so excited to see Tia Carla and
Tio Bruno that he forgot all about his notebook.
He left it on the plane.

Chapter 2

A Lucky Find

It was very quiet on the plane when all the passengers had got off. But then the cleaners came on board and it was noisy again. The noisiest cleaner of all was Vera.

"The best part of my job is cleaning out the seat pockets!" said Vera loudly.

She started cleaning row 9.

"It's amazing what people leave behind!"
Vera laughed.

But she was so busy chatting that she forgot
to clean out the pocket in front of seat 9B.

New passengers soon came aboard.
A man with a big bushy beard sat in seat
9B with his daughter, Anya, next to him.
They were travelling back to their home
in the Netherlands.

Soon after take-off, it was lunchtime, but Anya didn't like the food. She couldn't wait to eat her favourite apple pancakes when she got home. She thought about the cafe in the town square she went to every Sunday with her dad. She smiled when she remembered the bells of the town clock near the cafe, and the smell of flowers from the flower market.

"You're daydreaming, Anya!" said Dad.
"You've spilled your juice!"
He looked for a tissue in his seat pocket.
But what he found wasn't a tissue.

"Ooh!" said Anya.
"That's somebody's notebook.
Can I see it?"

Anya read about Ernie the Explorer. "So Peru is the most special place EVER, is it?" she thought. "Well, it's time Ernie took a trip to *my* country!"

Anya took out some pencils from her bag and started writing with a **sparkle** in her eye.

The most special place EVER!
by ANYA

Ernie the Explorer went to the Netherlands and found his three favourite things.

1) A **bicycle** ride!

Ernie cycled through the countryside, watched the windmills and spotted a stork.

Nice nest!

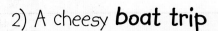

2) A cheesy **boat trip**

Ernie went on a boat trip on the canals and tried the local cheese.

Tasty cheese!

3) A **stroll** in the city

Yum!

Ernie saw beautiful tulips in the flower market. Then he ate some delicious apple pancakes, and listened to the bells of the town clock.

Ernie's Trip Rating:
The Netherlands is **FANTASTIC!**

Chapter 3
More Adventures

Hours later, Anya and her dad arrived back in the Netherlands. Before Anya got off the plane, she slipped the notebook into her bag.

The airport was bustling with people. Suddenly, a boy bumped into Anya and their bags tumbled to the floor.

Quickly, the two children picked up everything. Anya rushed off in one direction, and the boy, Themba, rushed off in another direction.

Themba was travelling home to South Africa with his grandma.

"Can I have my football sticker book?" asked Themba, once they were seated on the plane.

"It's in your backpack in the overhead locker," replied Grandma. "I can't get it now because the seatbelt sign is on."

Themba waited impatiently to add his new stickers of his favourite team.

Themba looked at his stickers of the players in their bright shirts. He remembered his own football shirt hanging in his wardrobe at home. He wore it when his sister took him to a match in a big stadium. The crowds were so noisy, blowing their horns and cheering. That time, his team won! It was the best day ever!

When Themba finally got his backpack, he had a big surprise. "How did this get here?" he wondered, looking at the notebook.

He read all about Ernie the Explorer.

"Ernie had better get ready to go again!" Themba thought. And so he began to write.

The most special place **EVER!**
by Themba

Ernie the Explorer went to South Africa and found his three favourite things.

:1: The **ocean**

I'm king of the waves!

Ernie enjoyed the sunshine on a sandy beach, watched whales from a fishing boat and surfed the big waves.

2: A wild **ride!**

Ernie visited an ostrich farm, saw some huge eggs and rode the biggest, fastest bird in the world.

OSTRICH FARM

3: **Football** fun

Ernie blew a noisy horn and cheered with the crowds at a football match in a massive stadium.

ERNIE'S TRIP RATING:
SOUTH AFRICA IS **COOL!** * * * * *

Suddenly, the plane started bumping up and down. Themba was scared.

"Don't worry," said Grandma. "It's just a strong wind."

Themba didn't notice that the notebook had vanished. It had slipped off his table and slid along the floor of the plane.

Who would find it next?

Chapter 4

The End of Ernie's Adventures?

Two weeks later, it was time for Pablo to say goodbye to Tia Carla and Tio Bruno.

The family boarded the flight home.

"This is the **same plane** we came on," said Pablo. "And I'm in seat 9B again!"

Later on, Pablo remembered his notebook. "It could still be here," he said hopefully.

He looked under his seat. Nothing. Then he stuck his hand into the seat pocket in front. Empty.

Pablo was disappointed.

"Never mind," said Mum. "It's late, get some rest."

But Pablo couldn't sleep – the man in front was talking too loudly.

"What's he saying?" thought Pablo, peeping over the seat.

"Read this!" the man said to his friend. "It's fantastic! I agree with Pablo – Peru is amazing!"

The man was holding Pablo's notebook!

"I'm Pablo!" Pablo cried. "*I* wrote that!"

"You weren't the only one who wrote in here," said the man, passing Pablo the notebook. "Look!"

"Anya and Themba? Lara and Aran?" read Pablo. "Hey! Who said they could write in my notebook?"

"Can you read it to me?" asked Lola, snuggling up to him. "Pleeease?"

"OK," said Pablo, and he read the adventures of **Ernie the Explorer** to his little sister.

"Wow! Look at all the places Ernie has been! He's been sledging in Austria and visiting beaches in Thailand! He's explored some amazing places!"

"Pablo," said Lola, "are you going to take your notebook home?"

Pablo thought for a moment. Then he put the notebook in the seat pocket in front.

"No," he said. "Ernie still has many more special places to explore!"